On the Way to Palermo

This edition is limited to
five hundred numbered copies,
of which this is Number

37

For John! With warm greetings

On the Way to Palermo

and other poems

by

Aaron Kramer

With an Introduction by
Clinton W. Trowbridge

South Brunswick and New York: A. S. Barnes and Company
London: Thomas Yoseloff Ltd

© 1973 by A. S. Barnes and Co., Inc.

A. S. Barnes and Co., Inc.
Cranbury, New Jersey 08512

Thomas Yoseloff Ltd
108 New Bond Street
London W1Y OQX, England

Library of Congress Cataloging in Publication Data

Kramer, Aaron, 1921–
    On the way to Palermo.

    "Limited to five hundred numbered copies."
    I. Title.
PS3521.R2905   811'.5'4   70-146761
ISBN 0-498-07845-0

Printed in the United States of America

FOR KITTY

the star by which I travel
and the ballast that brings me home

Contents

Acknowledgments   11

Introduction by Clinton W. Trowbridge   13

Notes   21

My Father's Ghost   25
Sister   26
The Last Time I Ever Was Carried   27
Depression   29
Phone Call   29
The Death of a Dog   30
In the Parking Lot   31
The New Day   33
Morning   34
Homecoming   34
The Favor   35
Suddenly I Find Myself   36

Daybreak   39
Reading to a Child   41
Subway Carving   42
Domestic Scene   42
Department Store   44
Hymn   45
A Drowning   47

7

A Life Sets   47
Adventure   48
The Circle   49
On Windy Noons   50
Moving Away   51
Old Couples   52
Cadenza   53
Combing   54

• •

Overpasses   59
Spring Song   60
To Dream of Bridges   62
The Doll   62
Joy   63
Carpeting Day   64
His Something   65
Nocturnes   65
    1. Sullenly, without conviction, the rain
    2. There must be some sense in my coming awake
    3. This happened in the deep of night one night
    4. Between the disappearance of the secret formula
    5. Back in the room where the breathing is
    6. On the first night of their twenty-ninth year of marriage

• •

Visions   73
Border Incident   73
Not Being Yevtushenko   75
To the Countrymen of Alfred Kreymborg   76
Irish Lullaby   76
Rereading Robert Burns   77
At Night   78

For Melina Mercouri 79
Considering My Country 80
Newscast 81
Loyalty March 81
Henry at the Grating 82
Gypsy Moths in the Suburbs 83
A Ballad of Jesus 84
Dirge 85

•   •

Driving to Gay Head 87
Niagara 89
Wandersong 89
Cardiff Harbor 91
Air for Bagpipe 92
Night at the Concertgebouw 92
Tour 94
The Statue in Split 96
Sarajevo 97
Venice 98
Taormina 99
On the Way to Palermo 100
A Good Buy 109
After the Tour 111

Acknowledgments

to *Adelphi Quarterly* for "A Ballad of Jesus," "Considering My Country," and "Newscast"; *Arion's Dolphin* for "Gypsy Moths in the Suburbs"; *Bitterroot* for "At Night," "The Death of a Dog," "Nocturnes: III," and an excerpt from "On the Way to Palermo"; *Broadside* for "Henry at the Grating"; *Carleton Miscellany* for "A Good Buy," "Adventure," "A Life Sets," "Depression," and "Overpasses"; *Fiddlehead* for "Driving to Gay Head"; *Jewish Currents* for "The Last Time I Ever Was Carried"; *Kansas City Star* for "The New Day"; *Lyric* for "Cadenza," "Daybreak," "Rereading Robert Burns," and "To Dream of Bridges"; *Lyrismos* for "Air for Bagpipe," "Joy," "Loyalty March," and "Suddenly I Find Myself"; *Mediterranean Review* for "After the Tour," "Combing," and "The Doll"; *Midstream* for "Morning," "Night at the Concertgebouw," "Not Being Yevtushenko," "Subway Carving," "Tour," and "Visions"; *Modern Poetry Studies* for "Old Couples," "Phone Call," "Sarajevo," and "The Statue in Split"; *New York Times* for "His Something," "Homecoming," "Moving Away," "Niagara," "Reading to a Child," and "Taormina"; *Poet Lore* for "The Favor"; *Renaissance Faire* for "A Drowning" and "Cardiff Harbor"; and *The Villager* for "To the Countrymen of Alfred Kreymborg"; also to the Folklore Center of New York, whose collection, *Henry at the Grating*, includes "Dirge," "Hymn," and "Wandersong."

Introduction
by
Clinton W. Trowbridge

The title poem of the present volume can be taken as symbolic of Aaron Kramer's own odyssey as a poet. Journeying with his wife toward Palermo, the narrator is almost stopped by the news that violence has erupted in that city. Though his wife tries to dissuade him, he must go on. Why? Because he sees this uprising as the beginning of a glorious revolution against tyranny and he is drawn to it in sympathy. Though he knows nothing of the situation, his imagination works him up to the point where he so completely identifies with the presumed oppressed that Sicily itself finally becomes symbolic of mankind, himself included, striving to be free. She is "a raw, convulsing heart / which should be held in the hand tenderly, . . . this planet's heart / my own." Yet, as he approaches the city, he sees that as a sightseer he is perhaps also one of the oppressors. It is at this point that he discovers "the truth of [his] . . . coming." Significantly, it is a truth he cannot explain either to Christ or his wife, but he accepts it anyway and even glories in its "bitterness." It is that he must lead the oppressed against the very tyrants that his own mild actions symbolize. So, in words reminiscent of Milton's famous sonnet, he declaims in prophetic outrage to those who would be free: "Avenge the murder of Archimedes . . ." Five lines, each beginning with "avenge." This is the two-hundred-line build up to the final twenty-two line, twelfth section of the poem. The first line, with its ironic allusion to Byron, immediately suggests that all is not what he imagined it to be. This proves to be the case. The "terrors of the headlines" prove to be simple peasants who have committed no violence and who only want "work, pay and—for their children—hope." Because of the language barrier, he cannot even understand what the issues are. Far from being able to lead them, he cannot even be of use to them. All he can give them is his love: *"bona fortuna"*; and when they smile in appreciation of his good intent, he suddenly recognizes their similarity to Mrs. Zappa and Mr. Cavataio, elderly Sicilians of his youth in New York City, figures of gentleness and good humor. The "scourge of oppressors," the Timoleon that he has imagined himself to be, is humbled. Yet, if he is not a new Garibaldi, neither is he a Roman conqueror. On the poetic level, if he is not a Milton or a Byron, still he is a poet and as such he can perhaps speak as a man to other men. His realization of what he is as a poet, and his acceptance of that role, is, then, the real fruit of his journey.

In "A Good Buy," the next poem in the volume, Kramer states even more directly what it is he has accepted. The punning title itself is a delightful hint. Through a train window the narrator glimpses two old farmers about to plant a field. Rejecting loftier visions he depicts them simply as human, though it is significant that they are part of a landscape of "overworked hills" and "Degas vines." He resists the pull of his imagination that might lead him to make some oracular statement about them and writes instead,

> I know only that they are there,
> motionless, silent, at 1:20,
> stopped in an attitude of prayer
>
> . . .
>
> awaiting you, as they awaited me.

In his foreword to *Moses*, 1962, Aaron Kramer wrote: "Mankind is perhaps worthiest of celebration when it struggles to set itself free. . . . This eternal defiance is my theme. Whenever it manifests itself, one feels like turning it into song." Kramer's concern with social justice, with man's struggle to attain his freedom, remains as intense as ever ("The Doll," for instance, is one of his finest anti-war poems); but there are only a few poems in the present volume in which he allows himself to speak out directly in the poet-prophet manner that characterized so much of his earlier poetry. And this humbling of himself, this modifying of his former revolutionary role as "scourge of oppressors," has forced him to a greater reliance on his craft as a poet as well as to a more personal approach in his poems. A good example of how his poetry has gained as a result is found in "To The Countrymen of Alfred Kreymborg." The poem rings with outrage at the way Kreymborg has been ignored by the "intelligentsia," but Kramer's passionate feelings are expressed indirectly, mostly through irony. Only at the end does he allow himself to prophesy, and his statement is all the more powerful for being contained in the perfect, concluding couplet to what we perhaps did not realize was a sonnet:

His faltering pulse, from Stamford by the Sound,
Across this poet-choking land will pound.

Kramer does not say that Kreymborg is as great a poet as Shakespeare; what he does is to suggest through the allusion to Stratford-on-Avon that history may well give him a higher place than his countrymen have found for him. He also implies that Kreymborg and America are one and that those who "nailed the coffin of his name" may well prove to be stiflers of creativity in general. It is a poem rich in meaning and literally prophetic as well for being written three weeks before Kreymborg's actual death.

"For Melina Mercouri" seems more direct, at least at first glance. There are "the citizens of my country" whom one does not choose and "the citizens of my heart" whom one does. Melina belongs to the latter. What appears to be a fairly simple comparison, however, turns out to be not so much a way of stating a theme as a vehicle through which the poet can treat subjects that go far beyond the comparison itself. Ironically, "the citizens of my country" are

15

vulgar, ugly aliens, living in an unreal, dead wasteland. Those who inhabit the poet's heart are twice fortunate, for not only are they all that these citizens are not but because of that are even hidden from them and therefore safer, more truly at home. The final quatrain both perfectly captures the humanity of Melina as she shows herself for all to recognize and at the same time elevates her, as Kreymborg was elevated, into a symbol of passionate and ultimately victorious life, the life and freedom that must come again for Greece herself, "the laughter that shall rise." The difference in tone, the new humility that I am speaking of, is most apparent when one compares this poem with "The Rebels of Greece" from the 1954 volume, *Roll the Forbidden Drums*.

II

Rumshinsky's Hat and House of Buttons, 1964, is dominated by images of death. Though the first poem in the volume tells of the poet's rejuvenation, most of the other poems dealing with the subject are ironically self-deprecating or contemptuous. There are numerous references to the poet's having lost the strident tones of his youth. "Threnody" is the most openly despairing:

> I harvest nothing, though the hayloft's fuller,
> and have no tune, although the day breaks loud.
>   . . .
> only the dream by which I lived is dead . . .
> And I, that bellowed so, must learn to be
> silent—except for this one threnody.

The volume shows, however, that Kramer was moving in the direction that he has now clearly taken; it was highly personal (as his earlier poems had not been, on the whole), and he was expressing his thought with more indirection: through his tone (often ironic), by means of apparently simple but actually highly symbolic narratives, and in general through a greater reliance on the traditional tools of the poet—simile, metaphor, symbol and allusion, in particular. "Rumshinsky's Hat" is one of the best examples of the new direction. We are led back to the poem itself for the answers to the question with which the poem ends: "Why should I then be, why have I been haunted / for three days by Rumshinsky and his hat?" Some of the answers are suggested in the proverbial joke the old man used to make to the narrator's greeting, *"Wie geht's?"* *"Man muss gehen."* The poem itself dramatizes for us why this statement must be taken in at least two opposite senses: "there is no avoiding death," and "man must go on in the face of death and other disappointments."

The volume concludes with a poem called "Nocturne." The affirmative answer to the question it asks as well as the rewards that follow the greater effort are demonstrated in the surer tone and the greater poetic strength of *On the Way to Palermo*, published seven years later.

> is it hopeful
> that I wake,
> grope, grieve, grapple
> for the poem's sake?

III

All the poems in *On the Way to Palermo* rise out of personal experiences. The best of them, and there are a great many, lead us through vivid, highly personal experiences to those that are universal. One of the most powerful is "Night at the Concertgebouw" in which the tourist narrator suddenly sees twenty-three of Amsterdam's "evaporated Jews" file in to occupy the vacant seats at a concert. After they have all entered and have become, ironically, indistinguishable from the live audience, in floats the figure of Anne Frank and the narrator is held in awe by a victory of the spirit that he can only envy. A dominant theme in this volume is, in fact, the overcoming of time. The poet, with his imagination, can serve as healer, conquering time both by dealing with that which is timeless and by fusing past, present, and future into a coherent and vital structure. A poem almost exclusively devoted to this "scourging of time" is "Combing," in which a grandmother, brushing her granddaughter's hair, thinks back to the time when her own grandmother had brushed hers. When she finds herself imitating her own grandmother's actions by unconsciously sighing, she suddenly understands that she has been able to link together five generations in love and meaning. Ironically, it is really not she but human nature that allows a coherent pattern to emerge. She sighs the way her grandmother did because she is joined to her in age and situation. Her granddaughter is having the same childish fantasies that she had when it was her hair being combed. The poet has done the linking through his imagination and because of his deep faith in the humanity, and therefore basic similarity, (not *sameness*), of all men.

Many of the poems concern warm memories of the past—of his sister, of his being carried when a child of three by his father for the last time—and, in these instances, the very act of remembering brings the past to life and in that sense conquers time. Even in the poems in which there is grief over a loss, even when that loss is the death of someone deeply loved, there is a kind of victory for life in the very intensity of the feeling experienced. In "The New Day" joy and sorrow are finally seen not as opposites but as naturally belonging together in one who has a basic openness to life. Even when the poet seems to be openly lamenting his own timidity and fearfulness, as he does in "Cardiff Harbor" ("Having attained, at the age of forty six, / a freedom from most of his hopes, but none of his fears."), he expresses himself humorously, and then there is the final victory of the imagination with which the poem ecstatically ends.

The real "scourge of oppressors" is the imagination, at least if you are a poet. It can conquer time, human weakness, can heal even our deepest griefs. Most importantly of all, Kramer tells us, the imagination can make us feel with others. It joins us to humanity. Empathy—particularly for the oppressed, the poor, the weak—has been from the very beginning the dominant quality in the poetry of Aaron Kramer. In one way or another most of the poems in this book deal with love relationships: with parents, acquaintances, lonely people, famous people, strangers, children, even dogs; most of all with his wife. "Suddenly I Find Myself" is one of the best poems in the collection and it is a magnificent tribute to the saving power of human love. Only Aaron Kramer could have written it. It was written for his wife to whom the volume is, quite rightly, dedicated.

One cannot discuss in a brief introduction all the ways in which a book as rich as this one delights the imagination and moves the heart. It would be a terrible omission, however, not to make some mention of the humor that runs through these poems. It is the cutting edge of his imagination, the mark of his voice. Nowhere does it run purer than in "His Something" and in so doing wrest victory from a vision of defeat.

In "Venice" the narrator prays, "Teach me how to seem a thing of air, yet hold." It is because Aaron Kramer has come into his full maturity as a poet in this volume, it is because he has relied not on the strength of his feelings alone but on the "shaping power of the imagination" as well, it is because of the controlled vitality and greater depth of these poems, it is because of these qualities that we can say that his prayer has been answered. *On The Way To Palermo* augurs *bona fortuna* for the years to come.

Notes

1) "Border Incident"—Six great Soviet poets are mentioned: Vladimir Mayakovsky committed suicide in 1930; Osip Mandelstam disappeared in Siberian exile in the 1940's; Anna Akhmatova and Boris Pasternak spent their last years in disfavor and obscurity; David Hofstein and Peretz Markish were among the many Yiddish writers secretly executed in 1952.

2) "Irish Lullaby"—The Liffey is Dublin's river.

3) "The Statue in Split"—Mestrović is a modern Yugoslav sculptor.

4) "Venice"—The *Bucentaur* was the state barge from which the doge annually threw a ring on Ascension Day, symbolically "marrying" Venice to the Adriatic.

5) "Taormina"—Empedocles, the great pre-Socratic philosopher, is supposed to have returned despondent to his native Sicily and plunged into the volcano.

6) "On the Way to Palermo"—The Conco d'Oro is a large coastal area of citrus groves between Monreale and Palermo.

7) "On the Way to Palermo"—The sounding of vespers in Palermo, on Easter Monday, 1282, signalled a general revolt which swept the French out of Sicily. This event is celebrated in Verdi's *Sicilian Vespers*.

8) "On the Way to Palermo"—Timoleon, Greek statesman and general, at the appeal of Syracuse's citizens, led a Corinthian army against the tyrant Dionysius in 344 B.C., and liberated other Sicilian cities as well.

21

On the Way to Palermo

MY FATHER'S GHOST

*"Do not forget. This visitation
Is but to whet thy almost blunted purpose."*

On the long sundeck beetling over the lawn
facing my woods as Hamlet faced his sea
I grow impatient with my father's ghost
which long since should have come to speak of horrors.

The words scrawled on my tablet are misfiled
somewhere, and probably illegible
by now: "Remember me!" I do remember.
Brushing aside three bluejays, brushing aside
my squirrel (like a clown on a trapeze
shelling nuts aloft a match-thin twig)
I do remember what it was.

                    He'd dragged
his breath through a heart-attack as through a blizzard
halfway to the el, and finally been found
crumpled under drifts of pain, mistaking

death's shadow for the shadow of whoever
might take his place at the machine, and shaking
for fear of that. Remember thee!

                                 Vengeance
was my idea, not his; nor did he, dying
or dead, enflame my filial blood. The issue
was, after all, no clear-cut case of poison
poured down his ear by some smooth-styled usurper
seeking his wife and job.

                         I do remember
how pure my fury was, how long it lasted
without the example of a Fortinbras
or a speech about Hecuba or a frowning vision
of him to egg me on.

                    Facing my woods I blame
their innocent posture, blame the blue they balance
on their collective fingertips, blame fifty
crisscrossing miles of villages and wetlands
between my sundeck and the el toward which
he dragged his breath as through a blizzard, blame
his affectionate ghost for probably coming on tiptoe
at night glad of my sundeck and my woods,
glad of my bird-feed and my squirrel-holes,
unwilling to damage my deep sleep for the sake
of that old fury which wasn't his idea.

SISTER

Girl of the golden thread:
you led me forth,
you took me in.

Nine months' grappling in the labyrinth
against the horn of lonely hungering.
You led me forth,
you took me in.

This, you said, is a sunbeam,
that, a raindrop.
Stop crying, said your kiss;
I'm the mamma cat, you're the kitten.
How does the kitten ask for milk?

Come, said your left hand to my right hand,
and we crossed the street.
You led me forth,
you took me in.

Whatever else has happened since—
miles of difference, years of difference—
still there is a leaning inward from two oceans
until our heads touch, as in the faded Sutter Avenue photo,
two grinning heads sharing a joke.

THE LAST TIME I EVER WAS CARRIED

There was a day with Aunt Becky and Uncle Mike
before the diaspora of Paterson's textile strike.
When it came to pass
that there would be no more fooling around on the grass,
making of silly sounds,
blowing of rainbow-rounds,
I remember being hugged in a way that left no doubt,
and showering goodbyes, taking home an affectionate shout.

The sun, with a lingering kiss for the westward-facing flowers,
moved toward his depot as we moved toward ours.
From the train, till Paterson was out of sight,
I watched the roofs turn into creatures of night
and wished there were a way to crowd every beautiful
and mysterious twilight cluster of gables into my skull.

After the trainride ended,
shocked to find myself in a pitch-black Brownsville, I
pretended
still to be sleeping, so that poppa, despite how big I'd become,
would not have the heart to wake me and make me walk home.
And I remember how, stealthily opening my eyes,
I watched from that strange angle the skies
with their billion stars bouncing at every step he took,
and window-lights all around . . . I wanted to look
everywhere at once, turn myself into a tremendous jar
and fill myself with the whole world's window-lights, and
leave out not one star.

This appetite, which I secretly nurtured at the age of three,
became, I guess, the impulse of my poetry.
Even now, although I should and do know better than to yearn
for twilight clusters, occasionally when stars and windows
burn
the old thirst rises: I wish to drink as deep
as on that night when in poppa's aching arms I pretended
to be asleep.

DEPRESSION

Our father came home once with two fists full
of coins, and emptied both into the apron
our mother wore, because the second time
she guessed which fist was fuller, she was right.
He helped her take the apron off, then carried
her stubbornly from room to room although
she kicked a lot and yelled: "Stop being silly
before the kids!" She was as tall as he,
and not a lightweight—but we wished we had
six rooms, not three, through which to follow them.

PHONE CALL

When I say Yes to Vivian
she hopes it means
Yes, Vivian,
I'm listening; or Yes,
I do believe you, Vivian.
But what it really means is
I remember.

Yes, I remember, Vivian,
the pink mole on your mother's chin,
your Paderewski minuet,
our giggling name-game
half that night in Brooklyn,
four cousins cooped
in one emergency bedroom.

But Vivian has more urgent business
than remembering:
she must, for the nth time, denounce
a vile world,
a stalking, plotting world
that circles her
with looks and laughter.

Too cowardly to murmur
Vivian, it's your imagination,
see a doctor—
Yes, I say,
remembering Vivian,
her minuet, her giggle,
her mother's brown-haired mole.

THE DEATH OF A DOG

To mourn for a dog, especially one whose breed
was mixed, whose only tricks in ten whole years
were carrying home the leash between his teeth
and vaguely lifting a paw after you'd plead
for half an hour with your hand beneath—
to mourn for a dog that frequently scratched his ears,
curdled the blood of neighbors when anyone knocked,
slept on forbidden chairs in his saucy mood—

to mourn for such a dog might be permitted
to lone, retired ladies whose lives were clocked
by his walking time, his friendly time, his food
and water time; but if your tongue has been fitted
for prophesying aeons doomed and born,
in silence mourn for him—if you must mourn.

IN THE PARKING LOT

Coming back
with my bundles
to the parking lot,
I was seized
by an insidious sound
the likes of which
I had not heard
for two years:

a sound
such as only the most atrocious
fiddler, playing solemnly,
or the greatest,
mockingly,
could duplicate;

a sound
such as the long-impatient
dog makes
to punish the calm
and stir the guilt
of his belated master.

It rises
not from the lungs
but out of some other region—
where sorrow festers—
and its rhythm
is the involuntary
spasm of sorrow itself.

Turning to the pole
from which the whimpering

came at me
I crazily expected
to see there
snarling with bitter joy
and fiercely hallooing with his rump-end
my dog.

Of course, this stranger
fastened to the pole
was also crazily mistaken.
Dogs are, after all,
supposed to know
their masters' stride
and smell—
not scratch with their sobs
whoever happens
to come from the market
with bundles.

Maybe the brightness of the sun
unsighted him,
maybe the auto-fumes
confused him;
in my case, though,
there could be no excuse.

For I don't believe in
a place
where dog-souls are tied up
or left to roam
awaiting the belated
souls of their masters;
and even if there is

such a place
I'm sure it won't look anything
like that supermarket
parking lot.

There was no sense
turning to the pole
expectantly;
no sense
driving out of the lot
with a strange dog's
misdirected rebuke
beside me and inside me
all the way home.

THE NEW DAY

It probably came of having been upset;
but I imagined my waking before the hour
was due to a burst of birds that never yet
had joined their forces in such choral power.

How dared I, after one brief slumber, forget
the dear friend in his casket, the casket in flower,
the widow eyeless, my own eyes blind with wet?
How dared I wake to a song as the soil to a shower?

So, wrestling against the sunrise at my sill,
beating back the fragrance that without warning
attacked me like one more regiment of morning,
I proved some valor; but the siege was brief:

the new day breached my wall, battered my will,
gashed me with pleasure . . . and out gushed the grief.

MORNING

Awaking to the golden cry of day,
I drink, like one distracted by long thirst,
my mother's melody, two rooms away:
her chopper's buoyant rhythm, and her burst
of cheer across the yard to Mrs. Schwartz;
and through my skull a warning rolls: "Lie still!
guzzle these ladies' greetings and reports
so gaily ricocheted from sill to sill!"

Then to the golden cry of day I wake:
my worn wife breathes beside me; two rooms off
the beds on which my children used to cough
are empty; I remember with an ache
that Mrs. Schwartz is dead; across the land
my mother chops one portion with slow hand.

HOMECOMING

Having both daughters at home does not give me
a very merry Christmas. Tall in the hall
they brush past mythic photos of their small
selves in camping days. Though they do love me
(in some new way now), it would ill behoove me
to fold them in my arms: satirical

34

silences from their scholarly eyes would fall.
Even their songbursts, their fits of laughter, grieve me.

Outside my window through the wide sky swarm
clouds that seem to know more than they are saying.
No comfort this night, when hailstones lash, to hear
both daughters breathing safely: what of the storm
next week? what of the storm next month? next year?
how will they be dressed? where will they be staying?

THE FAVOR

A wild idea: to catch her on the verge
of going, and say, "Bessie, would you mind
keeping an eye out for him, once the marge
is passed? There's little chance that you can find
him, but . . . in case . . . please, would you be so kind
and tell him that the girls have all grown large
and pretty and artistically inclined,
that even after twenty years the urge
to dial his number stirs from time to time . . ."

But at the terminal her loves in legions
around her sobbed; besides, it seemed a crime
to weigh a spirit down with such a task,
a spirit ranging unfamiliar regions . . .
and so she passed in peace. I did not ask.

SUDDENLY I FIND MYSELF

Suddenly I find myself behind the wheel:
exhausted,
going at sixty miles an hour,
sunglasses on.
But I can't remember putting them on
or turning the ignition
or getting into the car
or what exhausted me
or the use of this day's sun.

The trees
roaring east as if to contradict me
are a green joke
in a gray world—
like shrubs in a graveyard.
The west
should be greeting me like a great grim banner;
but there, too, an irony is forming:
a gorgeousness of purples
in the wake of the sun.

So I keep my eyes on the road.
I stop trying to remember what word the sun was
when it was a word,
what word *I* was
when I was a word.

Then, as suddenly as I found myself behind the wheel,
in the west she looms again,
the gorgeousness of purples
no more than a wallpaper motif.

Her face fills the west
and moves toward mine
at sixty miles an hour,
as if there were no windshield between us.

But I can't remember what happened
to lift her face on high once more
while my eyes were on the road,
while my soul lay under the wheels.
I can't remember
how long it was not there:
days? months? years?
or was it always there
awaiting the proper cloud formation?

Suddenly I find myself
soaring not westward but faceward.
It could just as well have been eastward,
but always it must have been faceward.
And every symbol on the dashboard
and every nerve in my body
becomes a word of a song
as my horn howls hallelujah.

Throbbing,
motor and man,
I plunge left into the passing lane:
lifeward, like Lazarus,
lifeward.

DAYBREAK

This morning through my bargain wall
there came to waken me no call
of breezes or of birds;
it was that ancient monotone—
an infant in its crib alone
beginning to make words.

I lay there listening with delight,
though not by any natural right:
neither its name nor sex
could I have told, nor do I know
whether above me or below
it rules two doting wrecks.

Still, by a logic more profound,
I'm licensed to possess that sound;
for, like a chronicler,
I could, had I been so inclined,
set down for future men to find
the facts on him or her.

My bargain wall did not restrain
that babe's initial roar of pain;
nor was my heart aloof
the night its mother had conceived,
the noons she'd craved, the dawns she'd heaved
under our bargain roof.

But while she dealt with limb and lip
I saw a cosmic partnership;
and while that infant's scream
received a nipple from its nurse
I heard a howling universe
all night, and could not dream.

This dawn, with biologic pride,
the father may have thought it tried
to shape the word for "Dad";
but unto me the newborn says
in known and unknown languages:
Awaken and be glad!

The DA! in German: I am here!
In Russian: YES! And in a year
barren of friend or fruit,
it brings to mind that Vedic chant
which Eliot once hoped would grant
rain, at last, to his root.

READING TO A CHILD

Your blue eyes
that still believe
cannot perceive
for what prize
I turn my lap
into a trap.

Since you yourself
truly care
how they will fare—
those princesses twelve—
you fancy I
am their ally.

But my concern
is not for them.
A subtler gem
I hope to earn.

A fortress be
your memory
to keep from me
mortality!

Do not erase
my voice, my face!
While life's in you
this hour lives too.

SUBWAY CARVING

Astride the toothpaste roar,
the snore, the electric leer:
    "Andy of Woodhaven Blvd.,
    Linda of East New York
    —made for each other"
        Were they pale? Thirteen?
        On their first ride together?
        Did witnesses jeer?
        Are they still near one another?

Atop the steel thorn,
the factory horn, the moon:
        discovering
        clinging
        made for each other—
    Andy of Woodhaven Blvd.,
    Linda of East New York.

Across . . . across the stars . . .
        But a chill invades the bone.
        Star-crossed
        across the stars:
    Andy of
    Linda of

DOMESTIC SCENE

One should be grateful for digestive need.
Several bathroom missions are guaranteed,

along with trips to stove, refrigerator,
cupboard. The mail won't come till later.
Meanwhile there's the business of lacing shoes,
fixing shirt and hair,
going down in the elevator
every hour, right after the news,
and grumbling to mask one's relief that the mail is not there.

When it is, however, and the day has far to run,
panic is the button one
presses, gets off at panic floor,
with panic key opens panic door.
In ambush on the coffee-table waits the *Times*;
in ambush on the rack, a Brahms quintet;
in ambush on the bookshelf, rhymes.

From eleven ten
to the turning of the key a little after five
there will be the problem of managing to forget
the problem of being alive.
Even if the meal is minced
into an hour-long affair,
what then?
—the last cup rinsed,
the last spoon laid away among the silverware . . .

In ambush outside the blind
a malignance of green;
in ambush outside the mind
They crouch,
offering to be considered, heard, and seen.
But no! one refuses to see, consider, or hear!

one stretches full length on the couch,
head aching, but clear.

And when, a little after five, the rescuing eyes appear,
one must not leap up, as a dog does for love and food;
one is not a dog, please remember, one must demonstrate
poise;
one must not behave as if there were something especially
good
about the sound of the key; one should perhaps even remain
motionless, as if the metallic noise
had not solved the lock in the brain.

Yes, but what of those to whom none shall arrive
a little after five?
It is this that makes one burn and freeze;
at last one understands
why dogs lick the hands
that turn keys.

DEPARTMENT STORE

With a pail of paint in your hand, an outraged grin
on your mouth, as if you have been
doomed for life,
you wander amid hell-bright adjectives behind your wife
(a bit like Orpheus, except that he
walked front, and must not look at *his* Eurydice).
While clocks in unison hammer years
away, she veers
toward the draperies, the silverware,

in spite of your despair.
You would give anything to be—where?
Bruges? Venice? But you *have* been there,
meeting with sick surprise
in the canals your own beseeching eyes,
demanding of miserable stones
a miracle for the dryness in your bones.
The planet's round; no matter how soon the jet
frees you, soon it will set
you down in the hardware aisle
to wander single file
behind your wife, with a pail of paint in your hand,
for that, understand,
is mankind's doom; and though each year the clocks will
pick up speed,
though each year you will yearn more fiercely to be freed,
you can, in fact, do worse—
as to your person and your purse—
than the well-stocked, well-lit bargain floor
of a department store.
You're not in a sickroom, not in a cell;
you must do something with your hands—it might as well
be holding paint. Consider it a nosegay. If between
the glove and shirt departments you by luck careen
against her lightly, why not see these aisles as groves
where dallying lovers gather shirts and gloves.

HYMN

Please, God,
be god

so I can
thank you
for being god
and thank you
for letting me
get a good break
on my dental work
and get an apartment
right near the park
and get all the channels
on my new t.v.
and get ahead
of Stanley in the office
and get rid of my virus
without penicillin
and get eleven
cards on my birthday
and get almost thirty-one
dollars' interest
and get even
with that bastard Charlie
and get beautifully stoned
on July Fourth
and get a nice tan
twice on the beach
and get you know what
once in a while
and mostly, God,
for letting me
get through with it
thankgod
over it
thankgod

in one piece
thankgod
more or less

A DROWNING

We weren't friends. I'd think of him no more
than twice a year. Now suddenly comes word
that like a god's hand shutting close to shore
the undertow has caught him. Since I heard
these tidings, daily on highways I caress
reddening branches through a drowned man's eyes,
hear through his ears the 7:12 Express,
take through his throat my coffee, with surprise
pick out a necktie in his natty fashion,
and—worst of all—(do not repeat this, please!)
the other night, in the safe swim of passion,
I felt an undertow suddenly seize
me; in her harboring embrace she wound
that other, while I sank and meekly drowned.

A LIFE SETS

The generosity of its high passage
and suddenly now these great cold jaws of its dusk,
remind me of the sun; but not the memo
instructing me how many traffic lights
to leave behind, nor the turbulent parking-lot,
the desk-clerk's metal tongue, the corridor prose,

the spring-burst hand, the nurse's laugh, the dread
beaming from eye-balls, my own dread reflected
where Byron, the Appenines, Brunnhilde circled
by magic flame, have hitherto been reflected.

Fact is, he's come thirty pounds shy—more than a fifth
of his total weight—within the past nine weeks.
Fact is, in spite of life-long principles,
he asked for the sweat-soaked bed-clothes to be changed
early this morning. His temperature reached a hundred
and five. Fact is, his appetite is rotten.

When a sun sinks, the entire firmament
is barely enough to hold its harsh red scream.
And, subtle as he is, he may have sensed
my disappointment; for, sitting bolt upright
he gasps of peaks now, poets, operas;
and, while the fellow in the neighboring bed
sleeps, or pretends to, while the time-pressed doctor
gallops over a chart, my kind friend plays
the metaphor to the hilt, and goes down shining.

ADVENTURE

Being operated on for the first time at forty-five
was one of my adventures.
Ordered to remove all dentures,
I laughed; wheeled in on a stretcher, I smiled
—knowing that I would be wheeled out alive;
that, compared to certain others, I had the health of a child.

For several days, since harvesting notes
is one of my professions,
I let myself swarm with anecdotes
and impressions
so that I could feel genuinely richer coming out,
despite the bill, than I had been
when going in.

There was, it is true, some pain to grumble about,
and for a while I was forbidden to drive,
but all in all
being operated on for the first time at forty-five
was what you might call a ball.

It was what you might call a ball, except
for the undertone, usually at night, that crept
in through the slats of the door
from other rooms along my floor
whose occupants were mostly older
than forty-five (though one of them was scarcely half),
and had been opened in more important places
than the left shoulder,
and did not laugh
about dentures, and had no smiles on their faces,
so pale, so thin,
when the stretchers wheeled them in.

THE CIRCLE

Headed for parking lot, bus stop, or station,
we see past the circle between our four buildings
as if past a planet we've nothing to do with.

49

Dentless, newfangled, an ambulance sits there
alongside a circle of top-heavy tulips.

High overhead, at a few of the windows,
old eyes reflectively gaze toward a cloud-break
hoping the sun will be good to their benches
where, in a circle, they'll sit through the midday
throwing no glance toward the ambulance, chatting
of anything else, as the careful old tulips
look straight ahead, never mentioning winds.

ON WINDY NOONS

Lately I've begun to notice
elderly persons in lobbies
on windy noons
who'd rather see garbage-men lifting barrels
than the glossy silence
of a phone,
photos of unknown grandsons in Seattle,
a wife much farther west.

If, meeting their eyes,
you mentioned the wind,
they would rush to repay you
with voyages, battles.
In the ripening sun
their eyes would gather courage,
as if to say:
Listen!
I was not always here.

I too hurried from work,
drove up to the door for a wife,
piggy-backed children,
lugged home a pair of lamps, a walnut desk.

But the sun goes,
and darkness seizes their eyes:
perhaps the time
whose witnesses cannot be called
. . . never was!
perhaps the time without witnesses
is here already
. . . invisibility!

Lately
on windy noons
they've grown visible to me,
though I don't yet meet their waiting eyes.

MOVING AWAY

When I confessed
that moving away from town
had left me lonely
all at once he raised his head
and turned it to one side
like an antlered thing
surprised
by the crackling of a twig.

Nights later

wakened by what sounded like a shot
I thought of his children
at distant colleges
his wife chosen by cancer
his father fading from the ancestral street
his term of lordship ending at the office
his hope for man transformed into a smirk
all moving
moving away
as I had moved across two county lines
only further, further.
And I knew that my word *lonely*
had reached him in his fastness
like the report of an approaching gun.

OLD COUPLES

Old couples in the act of lovers
remind me of a goldfish pair;
but not because the darkness covers
a humdrum, fishlike stare.

No—it is that their mouths resemble
furiously respiring fish
that rise from time to time atremble
and fill their gills afresh.

Separately rising, loneward sinking,
the creatures of the sea inhale;
while humans drink each other's drinking
without which they would fail.

CADENZA

During the slow movement of the Brahms sonata
my gaze, wandering from the violin,
alit on the bare, ripe shoulder of my neighbor
who'd made us all rise when she tardily came in,

the one whose violent yawn had outraged
Beethoven, the graying one, lumpy-faced,
who evidently had accepted the ticket
of a cousin rather than let it go to waste.

Precisely at that moment of deepest introspection
I watched, like a paralyzed witness to a crime,
five fingers surreptitiously top the horizon
and crawl down her arm in perfect time.

So—he was hers, the fat, seedy fellow
beside her, the short one, the one with baldy pate
and moth-eaten whiskers; no question about it:
here came the sure-footed fingers of a mate!

Ten days have passed since the concert; I remember
nothing of the music except that it was slow—
but I do remember very well the nausea, the wonder
with which I saw his digits familiarly go,

and once again I am swept by awe, by revulsion
at thought of those fingers turning that arm's
silence into song, as if he were the fiddler
and out of her pulse he was pulling Brahms.

Hers! who had made us all rise in our places,

whose face was lumpy, whose hair was half-gray,
who had yawned down the roar of Beethoven boldly,
whose cousin had given her ticket away.

COMBING

Though the smile (with which at first
she bent over her granddaughter's hair
as if it flowed to satisfy a thirst)
is still there—

and although her combing hands
still magically, stroke by lyric stroke,
wake the fire among those curling strands
they then woke—

now the smile's a frozen curve;
out of no golden fountainhead she drinks.
Her hands efficiently, but blindly serve
while she thinks.

* * * *

One afternoon I came
to visit grandma knitting on her porch
uptown. She let me have a comb;
and, settling on my perch
in back of her,
slowly I stroked her hair.

The strands began to flare,
wave after wave, until they seemed about
to make a gold flood on the floor
in which, without a boat,
I might have drowned
unless the gold were drained

or fishermen (who cast
their net for golden mackerel and carp,
by golden mermaids lulled and kissed,
gold shells given to keep)
before the night
would catch me in their net.

* * * *

Of all, later that year,
who crowded round her shroud,
only four
Christmas card cousins (if they were
to mention grandmother) remain to laud
her famous rendering of the Schubert serenade.

And the impersonal stare
with which she suddenly weighed
my combing of her,
nests only in one mind, no more—
the same which nests the mysterious sigh she sighed
while merrily I rode her golden-billowing flood.

So . . . *she was born in 1839.*
If this girl lives to be seventy-two as well,
we'll have embraced a bicentennial span
with me the pivot, this day pivotal . . .

—At first such reckoning caused her cheeks to exult:
she had been blessed with a power, a privilege!
Immortal breezes fondled her; she felt
herself a firm link between age and age,

as if she hung midway in a ravine
with left hand clutching grandma's time by the hair
and with right hand her grandchild's. But the chain
of memory thickened past the porch, the bar

of Schubert *lied*—accruing illnesses,
weddings, a quarrel (guessing, from what she now knew,
much more)—weighed down by voices, faces, days
of great-aunts, names of neighbors, shapes of snow

on nowhere undemolished elm and gable
but in her sudden glimpse. It was too much
for one person to hold. It bent her double.
The smile died. She swayed there in a gulch

between Past and Future—but they glowered apart
too fast—the Future fell away. Vainly
the right hand grasped: her grandchild's curls were short!
Would she know peace or turmoil? would she grow queenly

or wretched, or at all? would her world prosper? . . .
But as the infant strands slipped from her, those
of grandmother wound round as if to clasp her.
And she, who'd clung so proud, felt herself lose

the privilege. Wider and wider yawned
the chasm her two loving arms had spanned.
And grandmother's ferocious hair wound round
her frail left wrist, dragging her underground.

* * * *

Yet all at once she achieves (though unaware)
the timeless grip from which she feels herself riven:
turning upon the child in its high chair
the same mysterious sigh, the impersonal stare
given
by an old face in 1847
into a grandchild's care
who, dreaming of silver fishermen, drove through the silver
hair.

OVERPASSES

Even now, especially through colored glasses,
certain overpasses
turn into entryways of fortresses
or palaces
unless I keep in mind
how dreamlessly they were designed,
how gracelessly cemented:
like props rented
for a second-rate opera stage—
somewhat smudged, slightly dented,
the Gothic or Romanesque age
thoroughly misrepresented.

Although I know enough of ancient places
not to imagine traces
of battle or expect portcullises
suddenly to drop between me and the kisses
of a pale princess,
nevertheless

especially through colored glasses
certain overpasses
—the ones with arches—
even now turn into entryways; an army marches
out, and at their heel
gallops my automobile . . .

Having, of course,
mastered the difference between horse
and Buick, mildly I maintain
a speed of fifty in the center lane.
But when I catch, out of the corner of my eye,
children on their way from class
coming by
over the overpass
nothing can utterly convince
me that they are less
than princess
and prince.
My childhood wells up in my throat:
I envy the armor in their ancestral hall,
the ivy on their wall,
the battlements reflected in their moat.

SPRING SONG

I shall not, do you hear, be trapped again.
Astride a sunray, if you like, slide in
to where I crouch, tight-fisted. Enlist my glance,
if you like, on behalf of your crafty dance;
muster all your art

to rouse my heart
and wind it, willing or no, into the valse,
and like a clock rewind its pulse.

Though my feet follow you down the stair,
though your breeze-fingers seduce my hair,
though ears yield to your thrust of sound
and lungs be drowned
in your Atlantic air,
I shall not be trapped again, do you hear.

I shall not be deluded by the news
of a milding trend. I shall refuse
the messages of buds.
I shall see through the harmless looks of clouds.
I shall wrap something better than a coat
around nostrils, nerves, and throat.
I am not a schoolboy, this is not my first
trial, I shall knock down your pitcher, I shall not be betrayed
                                        by thirst.

See my fists, they are too tight
even for you to open. You shall not get the hemp of blight
away from me this time, though the palms of my hands be
                                        torn
with the clutch and the tug of it. I scorn
the red silk, the green cotton you offer in its stead.
Blight is the hemp I shall wear at work and in bed.
Blight is the hemp I have wound around the moon, and
                                        wrapped
around the sun. I shall not, do you hear, again be trapped.

TO DREAM OF BRIDGES

I read of a bridge designed to span
a stream somewhere at the world's exotic edge;
and since it is to be the longest of its kind
merging two shores of man,
I catch my mind
enflamed, my spirit lifted by the lift of the bridge.

Where's my accustomed vigilance? Could I forget
that a bridge grows long, but agony longer yet?
that every river bank it couples with another
may send across the familiar contagion of a brother?
—I must be watchful, must beat down such dreams
as this, this subtle one of bridges vaulting streams.

THE DOLL

Beside the road,
entrenched
in mud,
fists clenched
as if by pain,
as if blood
rather than rain
drenched
the place,
a naked doll
face
down

lies where she fell
far from town.
What field of clover,
what fondling lover
fills that skull?
Grateful
I am that none has thought to move her,
that none has turned over
this form without cover
which lies
pounded by the skies.
I wish to think she is dreaming;
I do not wish to see rain streaming
onto open eyes
that gleam without meaning,
onto open
lips that have never spoken
but now are screaming.

JOY

O up from the parquet floors the blessings bloom,
and lotus eaters might loll in the living room,
and the balcony catches the soaring of the sun,
and heating, cooling, at last are centrally run.

O the movie's a merciful lighthouse minutes away,
and shopping's as quick as picking hors d'oeuvres off a tray,
and usually there's a spot on the volley-ball team,
and the Sunday Times is delivered while we dream.

63

O someone said something that somehow sounded like praise,
and tires nor teeth have needed fixing for days,
and three of the neighbors say "Hi!" in a tone that's sincere,
and I've fallen asleep almost every night this year.

CARPETING DAY

The day the wall-to-wall carpeting was installed,
he might have somersaulted, rolled;
instead he took
his shoes off and trod gently forth and back
across his acreage—east,
north, west—uprooting whatever disgraced
the landscape, which from foyer
to piano-room he eyed like a pleased squire.

The day the wall-to-wall carpeting was installed,
he thought of three rooms, cramped and cold:
he and a sister
sharing, deep in their teens, the bedroom plaster;
and he wanted to wire his mother:
Fly in at once, and let us eye it together!
he even wanted to find
his father, and force his news through the hardening ground.

The day the wall-to-wall carpeting was installed,
thousands without doormats grew bold,
arrived, and moved
outside his drapes like wolves. He suddenly craved
wood, be it stained with beer;
he heard it under the carpet gasping for air;

he heard it prophesy
that, lacking the feel of it under his feet, he must die.

HIS SOMETHING

It wasn't as if the phone had stopped ringing,
as if no hand turned the knob of his door,
as if the postman of late had been bringing
messages to his box no more.

It wasn't as if what he'd drunk when younger
won thanks no longer from his thirst,
as if what food once reached his hunger
failed now where it succeeded first.

It was only that somehow he'd crossed a border
into the bleak, unbearing lands
from which his something, in wretched disorder,
fled despite the clutch of his hands.

NOCTURNES

1.
Sullenly, without conviction, the rain
slaps. A wind discovers
my window's fault
and shoves something through
as a hired boy shoves Grand
Opening prices under

the door. No orb gleams
but the clock. 3 A.M. A thief
and a copper, locked
in one circle, answer
each other's breathing; a plane,
disoriented
by fog, pleads for its path.

From the pillow I lift my head—not high,
but it is something—and wait for
the wind's next leaflet. This
I shall not crumple.

It is too long since my
head lifted so. Why should
one thief, one copper, possess
a whole storm?
The rain may not care whom it
slaps; I call the occasion
historic. So often, so
low overhead the plane
roars that it is
lost,
I begin to imagine
the roaring comes
from my mouth.

2.
There must be some sense in my coming awake,
some sense in hearing her clogged urgent breath
along with the insolent speech of the clock,
the wind's word thrust as through teeth.

ow clearly tonight his syllables press!
all my times he never came clearer:
tient as a pedant coaxing his class
repeat after him. Shedding my terror

do repeat, clutch at his chant,
s refusal to rhyme, the thrust of his rough
osody through steel and cement
if it concerned my waking, my life.

is happened in the deep of night one night:
'd risen from a dream, and glumly squatted
side the bathroom sink without a thought—
es open in the light, and yet benighted.
ddenly on the wallpaper each blot
came a crocus blossom; then he sighted
trademark on the hamper; with delight
witnessed that the floor was tiled, not spotted.

His eyes, his own raw, unbespectacled eyes
one strange hour had found their primal focus!
nce then he's prayed that some such hocus-pocus
ght take his other blindness by surprise,
t once from the night's deeps he might arise
d see his blotted walls give way to crocus.

tween the disappearance of the secret formula
d the paranoid's explosion
bed the rain;
tween the rush of interplanetary rockets
d the sweethearts' reconciliation
bed the rain

coarsely, nastily
at the window
behind his left ear
and for a whole minute
even while the chanteuse belted out
with that expertly sculpted look of pain
amour! amour!
it entered through the portal of his left ear,
coursed through every duct,
and formed an icy maelstrom in his stomach
till he moved closer to the set,
turned up the volume,
and warmed his nerve-ends in the glow.

Now the last program is over.
Through blinds tightly drawn,
through deep bedroom drapes
in jabs the rain
triumphant
having waited its time.
And he knows what it is.
It is not his kind of rain.
It does not cleanse and quicken.
It does not skip across umbrellas.
It is a coarse, a nasty rain.
It snarls at the lifted head of the Empire State Buildir
It ridicules the watts on every floor.
And he digs his left ear deep into the pillow
praying for sleep,
for those television dreams to start rolling in,
those rockets, those embraces,
because tonight the world-old rain
jabs mercilessly

t his bit of life.

.

ack in the room where the breathing is,
here half the bed is warm,
ough he slips by the creak-prone door,
voids the creak-prone crevices
nder the floor,
evertheless she stirs:
readed questions form
—like steam
rom a sentinel dragon disturbed in its dream.

s he to say it is no concern of hers
at fifteen minutes before
ither the elbow of the storm
ubbing against the pane
r a cry from the street
r something less easy to explain,
omething supernal
r infernal,
addened his feet—
gnited his brain—
y means of a strategy subtle and internal?

hall he say that like a chosen thing he stole
ut of the cave,
eft her to dream herself still the guard of his body and soul?
hat he sat down at a window, parted the blind,
nd, rubbing his legs, looked out upon a great white grave
hose absolute lack of sound and motion
ay bare in the glare of a streetlamp pole
laring for him alone, as if mankind

with one exception had been wiped out by a tidal wave
of the ultimate white ocean
and he, because he'd recently been allowing death to see
                                        into his mind,
was left behind?

Need he confess how, eagerly, he met
a silhouette
which suddenly leaped into sight
rending with one bound
the lack of motion and, probably, of sound?
how, had it risen from the ground
to a grand height,
had its shadow fallen enormous across the night,
he might have supposed that it was Death, exulting
over its triumph, catapulting
from one end of its pasture to the other;
but being six feet high at most
and stumbling somewhat on its snowy path
it obviously was not Death
but a mortal brother
engrossed
at that unreasonable time
in getting away from an act of love or crime
or getting back to bed unnoted?

Must he mention how, rubbing the blood back into his leg
                                        or the madness out
he followed the runner through the parted blind, and gloated
at his godlike advantage in seeing unseen,
until a doubt
arose: do strangers, summoned by the same mysterious power
sit this hour

70

rubbing mad legs at windows, wondering what the scene
may be about?
or is he, of the whole town's population, appointed to behold
                                        this landscape of snow,
this figure, hurried and lean—
to think, and think, till he begins to know
what the two of them truly mean?

Into a hallway or into worse weather
his brother disappears
not aware that they've been staggering together
for three full minutes. (Whether those minutes turn into years
remains to be seen.) He draws the blind, unfortunately
                                        touching the sill
with his knuckles. At once his ears
fill with the chill
of the silent snow. Back then to where the breathing is, the
                                        bed,
swiftly he goes. Pretending not to have heard what his
                                        guardian dragon said,
he pulls the covers of the cave over his head.

6.
On the first night of their twenty-ninth year of marriage
he wakens to the wind and other voices.
Back in his place he finds she too has wakened
just long enough to angle a bit closer.
His guess is right. Her hand's come closer too.
He folds it in his own. Soon, by her breathing,
he knows she's drifted away, leaving him only
her hand as a sister would when crossing the street,
except she's crossed already, her hand lies limp
inside his own, which rests—not daring to budge—

against unconscious buttocks. He refutes
nothing the wind can say; he recognizes
the full ridiculousness of his position—
once more reborn against a slumber of flesh!

VISIONS

When I was a boy I saw as a boy:
your burst of kilowatt, Dneprostroi,
hydroelectrified my brain
into a turbulent, turbined Ukraine.

In manhood I see the tundra night,
the taiga waked by a wandering light:
warmer than day my wilds become
at your incandescence, Mandelstam.

BORDER INCIDENT

They guard the border
but do not look like guards.
I tell them of a town
some versts from Kiev:
my father's shoes

echo on its stones;
his twelve-year-old shadow
is woven into its walls.
Some mattress retains
the groan of my grandfather
finished by fever
at twenty-four.
Around the corner
crouches the smell
of my great-grandfather's
bookbinding glue.
And it won't matter
if the lanes are paved over,
the walls levelled,
the grave-marks gone.

"We'll take you, but first
you must come with us,"
say those who guard the border
yet do not look like guards.
I know them, and quake.
I should, but don't want to
be wracked with Mayakovsky
unto roulette,
drink out of Mandelstam's
marah-cup,
be sealed in Akhmatova's,
Pasternak's silence,
answer the night-knock
with Hofstein, with Markish.
Slowly I turn
from my brothers, my sister,
and leave them at the border

which they are guarding
though they do not
look like guards.

NOT BEING YEVTUSHENKO

Not being Yevtushenko has its advantages—
although one envies his vivid arms and throat,
his large editions, interviews at airports,
listeners bursting to lip the hem of his coat.

Unknown in a dusk where even shadows are audible
beats being taken and tossed from town to town,
forever bellowing his bellow, forever
the same dance of his arms upbeat and down.

It is preferable to drink more than reflections of
one's own fine face in every passer's eye,
more than acoustical reverberations
of one's own cry, more than the bravo cry.

Not being Yevtushenko is better than slumbering
late, untroubled by matters of menu or rent;
the son of Pushkin, grandson of Jeremiah,
should be obliged to no man, no government.

TO THE COUNTRYMEN OF
ALFRED KREYMBORG
(written three weeks before the poet's death)

When one informs you that the cry-filled eyes
of Kreymborg are not yet entirely shut,
his rill-pure voice still trickling, with surprise
you shake assassin heads and murmur: "But
we thought the man was dead . . ."

                                      Aye—well he might;
long since, you nailed the coffin of his name;
long since, his song you buried from the light.
Aye—but his breath moves feathers just the same.

And let me add, while yet those feathers move
ever so lightly, that his lyric breath
more durable—in the long run—may prove
than yours, which feed upon a prophet's death.
His faltering pulse, from Stamford by the Sound,
across this poet-choking land will pound.

IRISH LULLABY

O'Casey in Devon,
Joyce in Trieste—
how could they rest?
Unforgot, unforgiven,
half-hell and half-heaven—
Liffey, the nest.

REREADING ROBERT BURNS

The voice of Burns, after long voyage,
halloos me as an obscure village
halloos its lad who chose in marriage
an alien lass
and in the far fields of his tillage
forgot his race.

The oak, the elm that used to shade him
have no hard feelings, do not chide him
for lofty promises he made them;
nor do the boys,
although his accent's changed, upbraid him
with darkened eyes.

It is the fulness of their greeting
that sets his guilty heart a-grieving;
a trophy he has long stopped seeking
mocks from afar;
long lost, a vision in his keeping
glimmers once more.

Just so, the voice of Burns salutes me
as in my childhood it infused me;
but though it never once rebukes me
for having strayed,
ashamed that alien bards seduced me
I bow my head.

And as I stroll deserted stanzas,
my blood recalls its earliest dances,
my legs desire to leap the fences,

my being yearns
to burst in rays across the plazas—
a son of Burns!

The roofs, I notice, have grown humbler,
the lanes less wide than I remember,
the wind less wild, the sky less somber;
but, echoing low,
my lost first song of flame and thunder
strikes at me now.

AT NIGHT

Headlong from my height
down the sheer hush of night
without one rescuing weed
—laughter, Schubert *lied*—
to lunge at: I am hurled
into the shriek of the world.

Headlong from my tower
down the sheer dark of the hour,
not one stalk within reach
—mate's mouth, Cezanne peach—
I am plunged, am drowned
in the world's bubbling wound.

FOR MELINA MERCOURI
(on the day the Junta revoked her citizenship)

I cannot choose the citizens of my country.
They chew gum loudly, memorize baseball scores,
watch underarm advertisements and horror stories
with the stare of those who walk into glass doors.

What, if anything, they think about the headlines
from which they quickly turn, I can only guess.
They're good to look at on the beach, the fairgrounds,
but behind the wheel they unfold their ugliness.

The citizens of my heart, however, are chosen
carefully. Here Jesus and Sitting Bull,
Sojourner Truth and Stenka Razin shelter—
all heroes in their time, all beautiful.

Sacco, Vanzetti; the miners of Oviedo
who hurled themselves like grenades at Franco's tanks;
the last Welsh bard, the last Jew of the ghetto—
who leaped, their banners round their feeble flanks—

such are the citizens of my heart, Melina;
you'll not feel alien among such as these;
you'll be made to feel at home by the women of Suli,
by the men of Thermopylae, by Socrates.

My countrymen are without imagination—
on a screen, a stage, they see your hair, your art—
or later, riding toward the hotel in a taxi.
They cannot see the citizen of my heart;

they cannot see that tenderly I carry
from place to place those cloud-devouring eyes
which weep so for the weeping of your islands,
which laugh so for the laughter that shall rise.

CONSIDERING MY COUNTRY

Considering my country in my time
where Truth is flogged and flowers are strewn on Crime
sons of a future century may wonder
what happened to the rhythm of our pulse:
did men rush forth into the square, and thunder
"The land grows fiendish, her insignia false"?

I set down this, a witness's report:
when neighbors met, they talked of rain, of sport;
alone, they plunged into a dream-like story
and were not waked but by the cries of clocks;
their faces did not show them to be sorry,
nor did their graphs register violent shocks.

But this is not to say that unconcerned
they saw the fragile spires our champions burned;
perhaps, like me, they felt within their stomachs
a welling nausea, in their hearts hot shame;
perhaps, while lullabied in August hammocks,
they begged the sky for Sodom's hail and flame.

Perhaps, like me, at every fresh disgrace
they vowed to seek some less polluted place
where, in the furious currents of a river,

they might rub loose the foulness from their lives;
perhaps, while spreading blue cheese or chopped liver,
they thundered prophecy at yawning wives.

NEWSCAST
(April 20, 1967)

First came news of the war: "our" bombs had struck
targets hitherto spared; with a clean-cut grin
one pilot described how "beautiful" had been
the raid, thanks to fair weather—a stroke of luck!
Homes had been hit (not many) but how else win?
Then came news of midwest tornadoes: a truck
flung on its face, children unable to duck
from the wind's road, hospitals caught in the spin.

I did not like to see that wind destroy
the open streets of a town in Illinois
—although from one of them may have sprung the boy
beneath whose grin the Haiphong streets lay broken;
I did not like to think some god had woken,
and leaned over my scarless land, and spoken.

LOYALTY MARCH

You should have heard them holler KILL!! You should
have seen them lunge by dozens from the line
of march, and fall upon a lad who stood
among the crowd, and kick his skull, his spine

81

because he said that killing wasn't good.
You should have heard them ram *"Die Wacht Am Rhein"*
down the world's throat. You should have seen how blood
can make the eyes of those who drink it shine.

Had you been here, you would not long have frowned
at their too martial step, too rowdy manners.
Out of your lips their anthem soon would sound,
and soon enough your hands would hold their banners,
and soon enough you'd help pin down some lad
among the crowd, whose traitor face is sad.

HENRY AT THE GRATING

I was not free at Walden Pond
although no man for miles around
was there to mock my somersault
or catch me running like a colt
or misconceive my evening song.
About my neck a burden hung;
no leap, no race, no chant for me:
at Walden Pond I was not free.

A burden hung about my neck:
the proud lads of Chapultepec
seemed to have emptied every vein
to keep the grounds at Walden green . . .
Is it not sickening, that blood
should quench the thirst of Walden Wood?

Is it not sickening that men
of Concord town, at Concord Inn
should clink their glasses and gulp down
a blood more manly than their own
and of these folk not one refuse
the beverage brewed at Vera Cruz?

In Concord town my burden swelled;
the stomach in my ribs rebelled;
from fresh-baked loaves I turned away:
was not their compost Monterrey?
Sick at the smiles of wine and bread,
by nothing but my nausea fed,
I found at last a public place
and vomited in Concord's face.

GYPSY MOTHS IN THE SUBURBS

When Truth found you out on your love-seats
behind the beer and pretzels,
you didn't bat an eye—
as if the gunned down villagers of Vietnam
would politely remain in their ditches.
Now the year has festered into summer.
Because you lend one another lawnmowers
and disinfectants,
I pity you by day
as you frown up at your darling oak-boughs
where worms multiply and feed.
But by night,
driving past your television screens,
I come into a storm of gypsy moths—

83

a white death—
a snow of teeth
against the lawns you dote on
more than other people's children.
Then I remember Egypt
and am glad.
Justice on high! hallelujah!
the first of many plagues.

A BALLAD OF JESUS
(Philadelphia, Mississippi)

Last night I gazed on Jesus
pinned fast atop a hill:
the moonlight froze upon his brow;
his singing lips were still.

And though I knew his silence
was more than man could break,
I asked him questions seldom asked
by dreamers when they wake:

"Why could you not stay happy
with hammer and with nail?
die old and fat, beside a wife,
instead of lone and frail?

"Was there a need, my brother,
to prophesy so loud:
to wake a hope among the poor
and terrify the proud?

"Was there a need, my brother,
to tell the mailed police
how touched with beauty are their feet
who preach the word of peace?

"Was there a need, my brother,
to die so young, so thin,
with vinegar upon your tongue
and iron through your shin?

"And must you rise tomorrow?
And must you die again
upon some other hill and cross
reviled by other men?"

Last night I gazed on Jesus
pinned fast atop a hill:
the moonlight froze upon his brow;
his singing lips were still.

DIRGE: APRIL 4, 1968

"The corn god produced the corn from himself: He gave
his own body to feed the people: he died that they might
live."   —*The Golden Bough*

No tears for the voice that never again will pour
ecstatic prophecies into our veins!
No tears for the manly stride that never more
will carry us calm through the eyes of hurricanes!

No tears for the lantern face that never again
will save us in boulevards of midnight creatures!
The voice yet floods us, the stride makes us men,
our street squirms, bared by the luminous features . . .

Sick! sick unto death so many years!
Sick in the utmost reaches of your soul,
oh promised land, it is for you we toll
the bell, for you the shedding of our tears—
tears, and a knell! Have we not reason to mourn?
Our king we plant, as in ancient times; but will corn
sprout from his limbs? are you able to be reborn?

DRIVING TO GAY HEAD

Which movie it was I don't remember. Anyway,
that's not important. I do remember how much
the people next to us, and we too, laughed.
In fact, we came out laughing; my wife remarked
that this was the perfect end of a perfect day,
and I agreed. But what was less than perfect
was the shock of darkness and oceanic fog
that with a single touch put out our laughter.
Grimly, hoping well of our windshield-wipers,
tires, and reflexes, we shoved off—somewhat
like middle-aged mariners—into the deepening fog
which was the sea's mouth sucking at Martha's Vineyard.

Was it for this, after all, and not those piddling
sideshows—harbor entrances, widow's walks,
superannuated harpoons—we'd saved for months,
mapped out intricate trails, driven to the ends
of highways and then some? Were all the cooing
tourist folders no more than camouflage,

small talk, with this night's journey the surprise,
the unmentioned bonus? Had antique shop, museum,
conspired to stun us, offering no example,
displaying no card to name or date this fog
through which our headlights crawled like a hushed couple
passing without relief, from time to time,
another couple masquerading as headlights?

Somehow we navigated the island's central
forest, half-resolute to shun forever
such fools' adventure, yet half-relishing
our feast of mist, visitation more ancient
than its hunched island. When we looked ahead,
fog stared into our faces; when we looked back,
there was total blackness, as if we had never disturbed
the night with our passage, as if neither road nor forest
ever had been, ever was destined to be.

And I, one half of a pair of wretched headlights,
measured my self in time and place more humbly
than at the curator's smile in the afternoon—
petted in the palm of my hand, savored on my tongue—
like some indigenous keepsake, some local taffy—
my new humility, a tenuous wisp
recorded neither on snapshot nor souvenir postcard,
and wondered whether it could long survive
this wracking ride, which half of me wished were over
while half would have liked it to go on till death.

NIAGARA

It was then broad day, I tell myself; in the sun
my hair and glasses almost too quickly dried;
afterwards we got back in; the ride
brought us into the dusk; it is over and done,
I tell myself; if I dared to step outside
right now, before me a strangers' road would run
across which neons flashing off and on
would plead with me to take some note of their pride.

Around the corner is not, I tell myself,
that mercilessly, immortally marched brigade
downhill, downhill, whether willing or no,
none ever, not one superb, insubordinate row
to slacken a moment before that ultimate grade,
to lean a moment over the edge of that shelf.

WANDERSONG

Next year, darling, next year
do you know what I wish?
I wish for a car,
a strong new car
that can waft us
over the border into Mexico.

To Mexico, darling, Mexico!
And what will we do there?
Why, we'll seek out Indians
huddled in their hills,

their ultimate hills
which only a strong new car can climb.

They hide, darling, hide;
and do you know why?
Because they do not want their children,
their scrawny, naked children,
to be photographed
by strangers with white round faces.

But we'll conquer them, darling, conquer them;
and can you guess how?
By holding out brotherhood,
a hand full of brotherhood,
and in the other
chewing gum for their children.

But when they test our faces, darling, our faces,
should we smile or weep?
If we smile, they may think us amused,
amused by the way their hut shakes;
if we weep, it may remind them
of the pillagers who came chanting pity.

And what if their mouths, darling, their mouths
are shut, and with their eyes
they chop us up,
chop us into tiny pieces
because we are so round, so white,
and they so hungry?

CARDIFF HARBOR

> The sunbird broke
> my blinds and spoke
> and I awoke
> at break of day:
> Tiptoe outside
> and hop a ride;
> you'll meet the tide
> two miles away
> where fisher lips
> command their ships
> to daylong trips
> from Bristol Bay!
>> Through blinds the word
>> of morning's bird
>> grew faint, grew blurred,
>> and there I lay.

Having attained, at the age of forty six,
a freedom from most of his hopes, but none of his fears:
afraid of waking anti-poetic sneers,
of catching cold in a city that sells no Vicks,
of yielding once more (or no more) to morning's tricks,
of hearing not Welsh, but a hard English curse on the piers,
he let the gulls caw "Dawn!" into his ears,
whatever was dross he let their cry transfix,
till Cardiff Harbor—glittering, flawless—appears . . .

> And there I lay
> at break of day
> two miles away
> from Bristol Bay.

AIR FOR BAGPIPE

From Carlisle north to Edinburgh
the way goes uphill, winding, narrow;
and on that road, and in between
the flocks of wool, the fells of green,
there rides and grows and sits unseen
the Groaning Bliss, the Grinning Sorrow.

NIGHT AT THE CONCERTGEBOUW

Center seats, hall high baroque,
program promising—
I've managed, managed it again!

This morning, amid the bright canals,
camera poised for every gable of note,
suddenly I was taken by surprise.
In his usual drone,
that had mixed together a hundred wisecracks, names, and
                                                          dates,
our guide made mention of her house
and every camera swerved.
But I managed,
managed to turn too late:
the building was drowned behind a bridge . . .
And if my wife remembered the name of the street,
she did not say so.

After the boat-ride there was more to see:
cyclists with streaming hair

92

among the trucks;
Rembrandt's house, of course;
an ooze of shoppers thick
along the Kalverstraat.
But we remembered to buy tickets for the night,
because at night . . . at night . . .

Gentlemen balding, ladies in elegant hats,
Amsterdam files in: mellow, untroubled,
not quite filling the hall.
Under Beethoven's probing
I begin to wonder
which of Amsterdam's evaporated Jews
might have bought the twenty-three remaining tickets.
At once they enter
—so easily do spectres move by night, by music—
and take their places: gentlemen balding,
ladies in elegant hats.
The applause at the close of the first half
fails to dislodge them.
During the intermission they wait in line
at the refreshment bar, the toilets.

Afterward, with the slow movement of the final trio,
she too floats in,
despite all my years of managing,
managing never to read a single entry
in her diary,
nor see the stage play, the movie
(though I did, by accident, one night
glance at Millie Perkins on t.v.)

In she floats, huge
over the heads of the audience,
thin arms flailing in time to the adagio,
the eyes in her Millie Perkins face
shut—whether in death or ecstasy—
filling the hall with her lilting,
chilling the hall with the draft of her motion,
the terrible air from her nostrils . . .
peering down at us, as if to say:
You are gray, you are fat, your teeth are in trouble;
I am fifteen until Judgment Day!

It ends; and she, at the first applause,
hurries out as if anxious
not to be jostled by the crowd.
Lustily I clap for the bowing, depleted players,
but cannot manage not to see her as well.
She mounts a bicycle,
rolls away, hair streaming,
disdaining the wild night traffic around her,
gradually indistinct
amid the dark canals.

TOUR

In four languages, the guide
explains as she has twice a day for years,
that we are entering
one of the quaintest sections of the city,
formerly the Jewish quarter.
Inside the synagogue she points out oddities.
"Notice the walls!"

Perfectly arrayed, as if being marched,
are names—
seventy thousand Czechoslovak Jews,
their dates of birth and deportation.
The calligraphers worked slowly, she explains,
so as not to be sent to the front;
thus the building and its chronicle remain.
Aside from this interesting fact
the room is bare; the group goes quickly.

I too wish to burst loose
as if from a tomb before the lid drops;
yet, summoned by the names so expertly lettered,
slowly I move, or am moved,
toward my destiny.
For this, instead of safe Copenhagen,
we came to Prague!
For this I was granted sight, a tongue.
Whether anyone brings me lunch or not,
today or next year,
I must memorize, memorize,
then hurtle into the ancient square,
open jaws wide, and howl forth a cloud.

REIMANN, VIKTOR 1892, GISELA 1887, EVA 1926,
         JOSEF 1930   26 X 1942
            ZIGMUND 1864, OLGA 1869 19 X 1942
            ANNA 1884, EDIT 1907   18 V 1942

A touch on the shoulder:
"Must you always be the last one
back on the bus?"
Meekly I follow, betray the deafening names

one of which may be mine.
Behind us the honeymooners from Pittsburgh
agree this was "a poor choice" for a tour.
A look from my wife—I hold my peace,
but it is costly: the madness
rushes into my legs, which tremble so
that I beg for the motor to start,
to spare me from embarrassment.

In her passionless, knowledgeable staccato
the guide announces
in four languages
that Hradcany Castle is next.

THE STATUE IN SPLIT

It struck me—because that harbor's curve
once beckoned Diocletian home;
because no eye tore at my skin, my pocket;
because of the ease between father and child;
but more because of the statue in the Square:
—imagine a poet in front of City Hall
surrounded by praising birds, by patriots licking ice-cream,
still pointing to his page, after four centuries!

It struck me—yes!
here one might settle, like Diocletian
abdicate all Rome!
So I wept at the pastry melting in my mouth,
the druggist's concern, the low price of nose-drops,
the sun revering each historic stone.

But as the sun went down that harbor's curve
a chill went up my sleeve,
for without warning I had come again to City Hall.
It was like catching a face between smiles.
There stood Mestrović's poet
locked forever in the tiny square,
an endless shrilling of beaks around his head,
Diocletian's northwest tower eternally eyeing him,
no one, none, not one of all that ice-cream-licking crowd
beholding what his finger implored them to behold:
his blazing page.

So my envy turned to pity
for Marko Marulić.
If he were not made of iron, I thought,
he could not bear it long.
And I did not settle in Split.

SARAJEVO

The point was to see the Wednesday market
brimful of hues—
not join the fezzes and kerchiefs
at the grating of the great mosque
through which one spied inside the garden
a dwarf towering amid the pigeons
that respected her bread.

The point was to see the Wednesday market,
not follow the dwarf
with giant lips and nose

pulling swathed feet
as if through quicksand
toward Sarajevo's stalls.

The point was to see the Wednesday market,
not capture with Kodak piracy
how at a corner, where four friends met,
she put her packs down,
clasped hands as they clasped one another's,
smiled as they smiled.

VENICE

City of Iago and Desdemona,
    broad canals and death-brown backways,
Norma's aria and slamming doors,
    honeymoon pairs and soldiers in packs,
Giudecca's squalor and super Lido—

city of proud by-street grafitti: "Yankee Go Home!"
    and on the Piazzetta, scraping: "Your picture,
                                            Madame!"
Burano's pure lacework of streets ("Oh, I could live here!")
    and the child, as she gives her name, unfisting a coin,
the gondoliers' manly talk among themselves,
    and their lunge for the boats as customers approach,
their noble stance at the oars, red ribbon flapping,
    and their whorish barcarole to flattered schoolmarms—

city of the Doge in his Palazzo:
    one Tintoretto-ear Godward straining, the other, earth

bound, in a tiny side-chamber, at the opening in a wall,
taking from a lion-mouthed slit the hiss of a name—

teach me, city (I came to play, but am praying)
what marriage is,
as I study your marriage of columns, arches, windows,
of cargoes arrived and sunk
of sailors homecoming and drowned
of Pellico and the Doge facing each other across the Bridge
                                                of Sighs—

teach me how to seem a thing of air, yet hold,
how to canal my tides and not be swept under,
how to marry myself to the sea
as you, year after year, amid loud cheering and low cursing
hurled your ring from the gilded *Bucentaur*.

TAORMINA

Over a bona fide
balustrade
built for the Spanish conqueror,
in a listening mood
I lean.
But the hour is silent—
except that
over my left shoulder
at the crumbled Greek theatre
clouds rehearse
unidentified dramas
while hungry behind me

Etna steams
for another Empedocles
and below—
far below the lush cry
of these terraces—
the sea
chortles and snorts
at the touch
of a half-built condominium's
German shadow
squatting
like a new conqueror
on its old billows.

ON THE WAY TO PALERMO

I.

On the way to Palermo stood, first of all,
Emilio Zappa's mother, a ruffled bird, under our window,
hands on hips, cawing her toothless good morning,
and Vince Cavataio's father
impartially gentle amid his family and fig-tree.

Next came Caruso
afire with Lola, false to Santuzza,
doomed by the bells of Mascagni's square:
Damon, despite Schiller's robbers and rivers,
thrashing his way to the gallows
to teach Dionysius truth;
Shakespeare's twins

bewildered in a harbor booming with cargoes, whores and
decrees.

On the way to Palermo
deadpan cinema henchmen, biting cigars,
poised for the decisive nod;
in ritual tabloid towns
clans warred over wooing and rape.

On the way to Palermo sat Aeolus
not a hair disturbed by the wildness in his cave;
Vulcan, ecstatic of hammer, half-visible through the sulphur;
Charybdis and Scylla, twins of untiring vigil,
each with its special trick;
the Sirens, so powerful in song,
Ulysses had to stuff his ears,
fasten his limbs to the mast, while sailing by.

II.

If the sun were on Messina's gables,
if grimness were not on the waves and mountains,
I might have simply crossed.
But sulphur was the ray that reached me.

III.

On the way to Palermo, mulling guide-books,
peeling maps, chewing time-tables, we sit
looking out seldom, and then
in hope of the picturesque:
a citric thirst pulls us, as Carthage
and Rome were pulled

to Marsala's sweet wine, Trapani's tuna,
Gela's cotton, Paterno's oranges,
the asphalt and cheese of Ragusa,
the olive oil of Messina,
the mineral waters of Termini,
the almonds of Avola;
and we hope to carry away
in the suitcases of our Kodak brains and intestines
whatever is Neolithic in Buscoli, Siculian in Thapsos,
Greek in Selinus, Arab in Buccheri,
Norman in Cefalù, Spanish in Augusta—
plus the rocks of Ognina, the stalactites of Mondello,
the legendary springs of Arethusa and Ciane,
the colors of the sea,
the foliage, beaches, panoramas, and air,
marionette shows, underwater festivals,
saint's day parades;
and around the corners of gaunt streets
(which, if quaint enough, we will also carry away)
pasta con sarde, sfincione and cassata
await the open shelves of our stomachs,
while painted toy carts drawn by costumed toy donkeys
await the shelves of home.

IV.

On the way to Palermo the *Tribune* cries: "Beware!
The South blazes! rocks rock the air!
Fighting erupts at Castel Volturno;
police are on stretchers in Villa Literno;
Molotov cocktails scatter the pigeons of Mondragone;
at Trentola they have torn a Roman Temple into barricades;

102

bankrupt at Casal di Principe are the windowframes of
                                                      banks;
directors attend a funeral of promissory notes;
no travelers' checks will be cashed today, my friend!
at Calatafimi, teargas or no, the roads stay blocked;
where shall the Mayor dictate to his secretary?
like tongues from his windows the insolent streamers flap!"

"Perhaps," sighs the wife, "we should stay in Firenze . . ."

Stay if you must, dear, with David's
delicate profile and genitals;
I'm for a David in trousers, lips roughly apart,
loading his slingshot with stones for a Roman temple!

CAOS! *Tribuna* bellows,
CAOS IN SICILIA!
TRAFFICO FERROVIARIO BLOCCATO
A SIRACUSA ED A PALERMO!
PARALIZZATA LA VITA NELLA CAPITALE DELL' ISOLA!
SIAMO ALLA MERCE DEGLI AGITATORI SINDACALI!

"Perhaps," she warns, "we should stay in Taormina . . ."

Stay if you must, dear, with the bi-weekly saint's procession,
stereo hymns in excelsis fluttering praises;
I'm for a march of crater jaws unlocking sulphur,
spokesmen for shrunken guts!

V.

Sulphur screams from Etna's
two hundred and sixty mouths.

103

Two hundred and sixty widows
beseech me
not to shoot them
in Kodacolor again.
When I ask how they came to be widows,
a sulphur silence issues from their jaws.

VI.

I should remove my shoes
and walk lightly.
It seems, on the way to Palermo,
that Sicily in fact is not a lemon
but a raw, convulsing heart
which should be held in the hand tenderly,
not stepped on or squeezed—
a raw heart, this planet's heart,
my own.

VII.

Scampi and octopus, octopus and scampi!
All night they nibble at my shores.
I am Sicily—what else?
Tremors—oh, what tremors!—every so often seize me.
From two hundred and sixty orifices
lava, like sweat, explodes.
Scampi and octopus nibble,
gods drop tears for the missing parts of their temples.
A busy night, a night without slumber. Cities moan.

And when, at two A.M., she asks, "Why do you toss so?"
shall one say that cities moan?

that Aeschylus' stage is laid flat to make room for lions?
that the pool in the anfiteatro thrashes with crocodiles and
slaves?
that Enna, whom Ceres blesses but cannot save,
falls to the Siracusans?
that Trojan Segesta, Dorian Selinus
grapple long and well at one another's throats?
that Rome sacks the one at last, Carthage the other,
leaving lone columns to mark their passion?

One mutters: "Scampi! octopus!
I was a fool to eat them . . ."

VIII.

Amid octopus and scampi, on the way to Palermo,
kids guffaw and splash.
She who hangs old clothes to dry
swells with new life;
three of her walls clutch
the fourth, beheld by Carthage eyes.
Amid igneous rock which sits like giant paws,
high-rise apartments ignore the craters behind them.
Peasants, stooping to their meager rows,
ignore the omnivorous breakers before them.
On the railroad platform, facing sea and sun,
atop a base of lava a flower-pot stands
from which a flamboyant geranium
sings.

IX.

Palermo, I saw from the outset
what your strategy would be:

the tourist office would be shut;
there would be no busses running;
nobody we met would understand us;
a window would open and a bag fly past;
beggars would tear at us with ferocious lamentations;
the hotel would be third-rate—no toilet-paper,
                              roach-marks on the wall.
You wanted to test me, to see if I would know you
despite your slut's disguise,
or ram your harbor, suck your female riches,
like all the rest.

X.

When those mosaic eyes had followed me
past the open confessional where a child whispered her sins,
past the eighteenth plundered Roman column,
past the cloister of unbenedictine meditations,
past the panoramic view of Palermo
raped for her golden gifts through every gate,
past the grim windings of Monreale astir with Arab ghosts,
past the great dry womb, the Conco d'Oro, emptied of its load,
past the phantom walls of Palermo
through which like a ramrod we tore
onto the Via Roma, road of spiked boots—
then I knew I was under suspicion
like all the rest.

And when I could explain
neither to Christ nor to my wife
why we were here
if not for the Baroque facades, the Neo-classic pillars,

the Gothic courtyards, the Arab-Norman campaniles,
the Renaissance fountains, the Byzantine mosaics—
then the time had come
for my own eyes to follow me,
because we were here for something:
a thirst drove me;
parched I stopped at every cross-street;
parched my eyes demanded of those we passed;
parched I listened to the silent towers;
parched I arrived at Verdi's prophetic statue.
—There, behind a screen of loose reeds,
loving the campari for its bitterness at last,
I discovered the truth of my coming.

XI.

Where do your ominous clusters ripen
for a new Garibaldi?
And oh you bells in all the towers of Palermo,
when, when shall you be heard?
The powerful expect you, at night they tremble;
is it not time, past time,
for Sicily's new Vespers?
How long amid the rotting corpses of trawlers
must boys splash merrily?
How long from bomb-halved buildings on the waterfront
must women lean, not bellowing,
but drying shirts and sheets?
How long, with even temper, must your donkeys
spruced up like courtesans in lace and spangles
drag miserable onions through the streets?
How long must none but Paladins
painted on carts

do valiant battle?
Where are the blocked trains? the swirling mobs?
I want to tell them . . . that they have my approval . . .
that their bitterness is my campari . . .
that if for their barricades they need another temple,
let it be Roman—what else but Roman?—I shed no tears
for Roman temples on Sicilian soil!

Avenge the murder of Archimedes!
Avenge the murder of your brilliant cities!
Avenge your noble isle turned citrus grove!
Avenge your ancestors turned harbor slaves!
Avenge your uprisen, pinned to the rocks of Lipari!
A Roman temple for your barricades!

XII.

The sun sinks to Palermo, Palermo to the sun.
The window-panes of City Hall stop blazing.
There at last we find them: terrors of the headlines—
gently peeking out of the Mayor's window
to watch us drink the slogans of their placards.
Six gather round, argue their case gently:
ten days they have stayed here . . .
what they want is work, pay,
and—for their children—hope.

We understand not much of what they tell us;
and they, how could they understand
that I am Timoleon, freshly arrived, scourge of oppressors,
in need of a city purpling with ominous clusters?

At least they seem to guess our love.

108

We shake hands. In wretched Italian
I wish them *bona fortuna.*
Their answering smile both parches and quenches:
it is not the smile of Etna, of Easter Monday, 1282,
but of long-dead Mrs. Zappa, hands on hips,
cawing her toothless good morning,
long-dead Mr. Cavataio, impartially gentle
amid his family and fig-tree.

A GOOD BUY

Oh yes, it was a good buy for the money.
To have eaten calves' liver in the shade of the Rialto
or veal, Genoese style, in the sun of Portofino
is nothing to sneeze at;
to have seen Chianti fields from Siena's tower
or from Milan's top spire a sea of roof-gardens
was worth the trip.

Listen—I can tell you what cafe to shun in Bologna,
what pensione to try in Taormina.
I can draw you a map of the Villa Borghese
so you won't get lost looking for the museums,
and I can reel off the bus-schedule for Pompeii.
Would you like to know where the most Tintorettos are,
the best Berninis?
how to say "toilet" or ask the price of gloves?

Listen—in Naples, about a block from the station
(ferrovia, they call it)
a ragged old woman sits all day against the wall.

In her lap are four pairs of shoe-laces.
She waited for me. She waits for you.
At 3:25, in Siracusa,
a guide at the Fountain of Arethusa
(he has a crew-cut and dark-rimmed glasses)
leans toward the most promising turista
and murmurs: "Your skin is like magnolia."

In a bit of field between Verona and Vicenza
(as the Venice express roars by)
a castle shell far off, fresh baby linen on a nearby line,
two old men together stoop,
broad hats close and parallel,
fingers earthward, tactful, knowing,
at the start of a long row.

What hour did they begin? how far
will they get by nightfall? what
was their ancestors' fate? what hope
have they for their descendants?
what have they ever said? what
does one prepare to tell the other?

I know only that they are there:
motionless, silent, at 1:20,
stooped in an attitude of prayer
or sharing a tableau, consciously composed,
along with the overworked hills beyond
that once were mountains,
along with the lines of ballerina vines—
petite, Degas vines,
holding hands, poised—
awaiting you, as they awaited me.

AFTER THE TOUR

Somehow, after twenty-one days,
the key still fit the lock;
but I was too full, too empty for subtle surprises.
Only now, moving from room to room,
putting out the lights,
do I contemplate the strangeness.
Twenty-one days of palazzi
have, naturally, transformed my living-room . . .
not that I like it less, or am ashamed
to find the floors wooden rather than tiled;
it is, simply, different . . .
as the stove is different
after Livia's kitchen on the Palatine,
as the bathtub is different
after Caracalla,
as the desk is different
after Mrs. Browning's in Casa Guidi,
as the panels are different
after Monreale,
as the street below is different
after Venice . . .
and, finally, the bed, my wife upon it,
my arm around her,
we too—till when I cannot say,
in what way I am not sure—
are different
after the sarcophagus in the Villa Julia
atop which, bliss in their orbless terracotta eyes,
recline the young Etruscan and his bride.